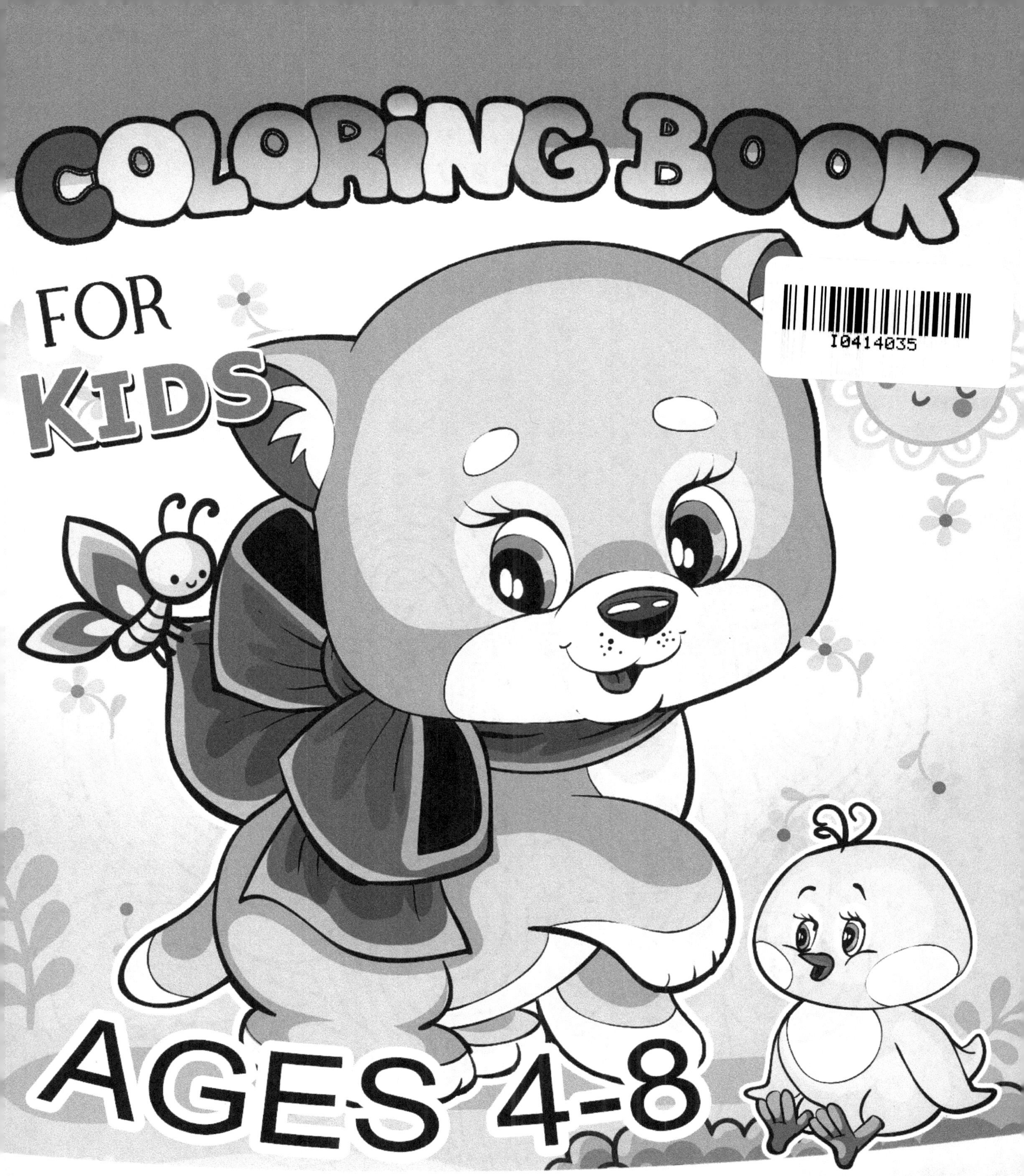
COLORING BOOK
FOR
KIDS
AGES 4-8

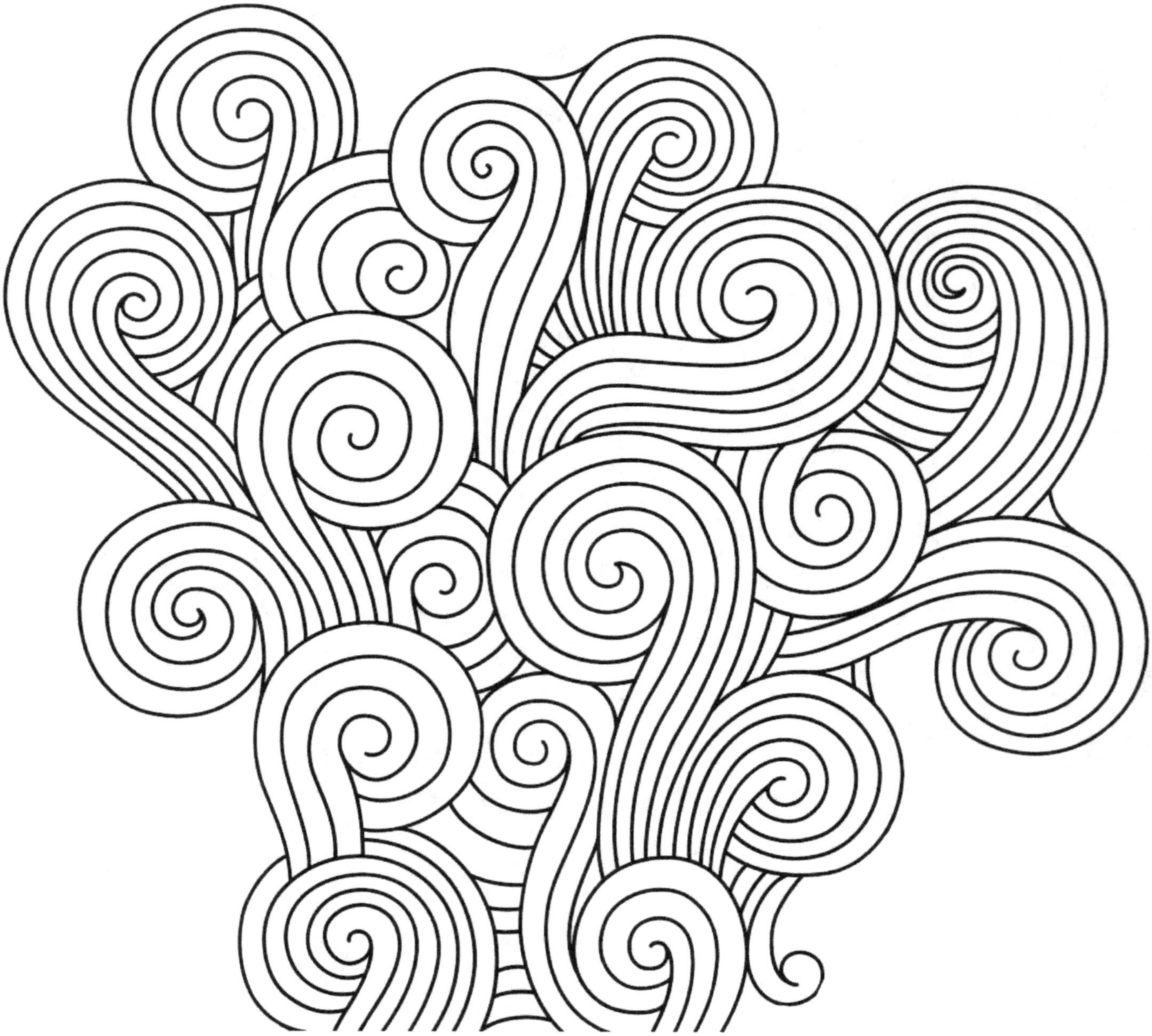

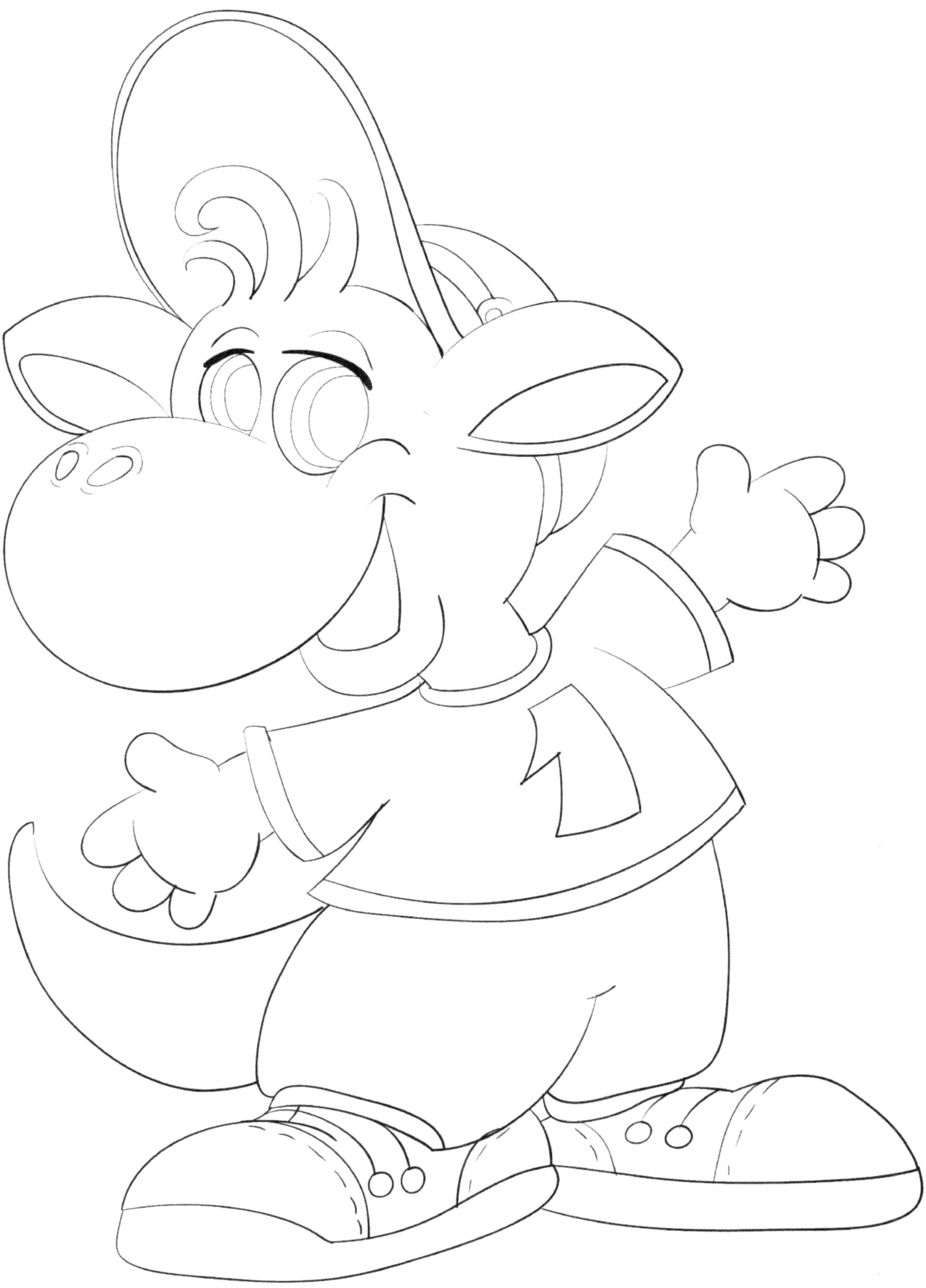

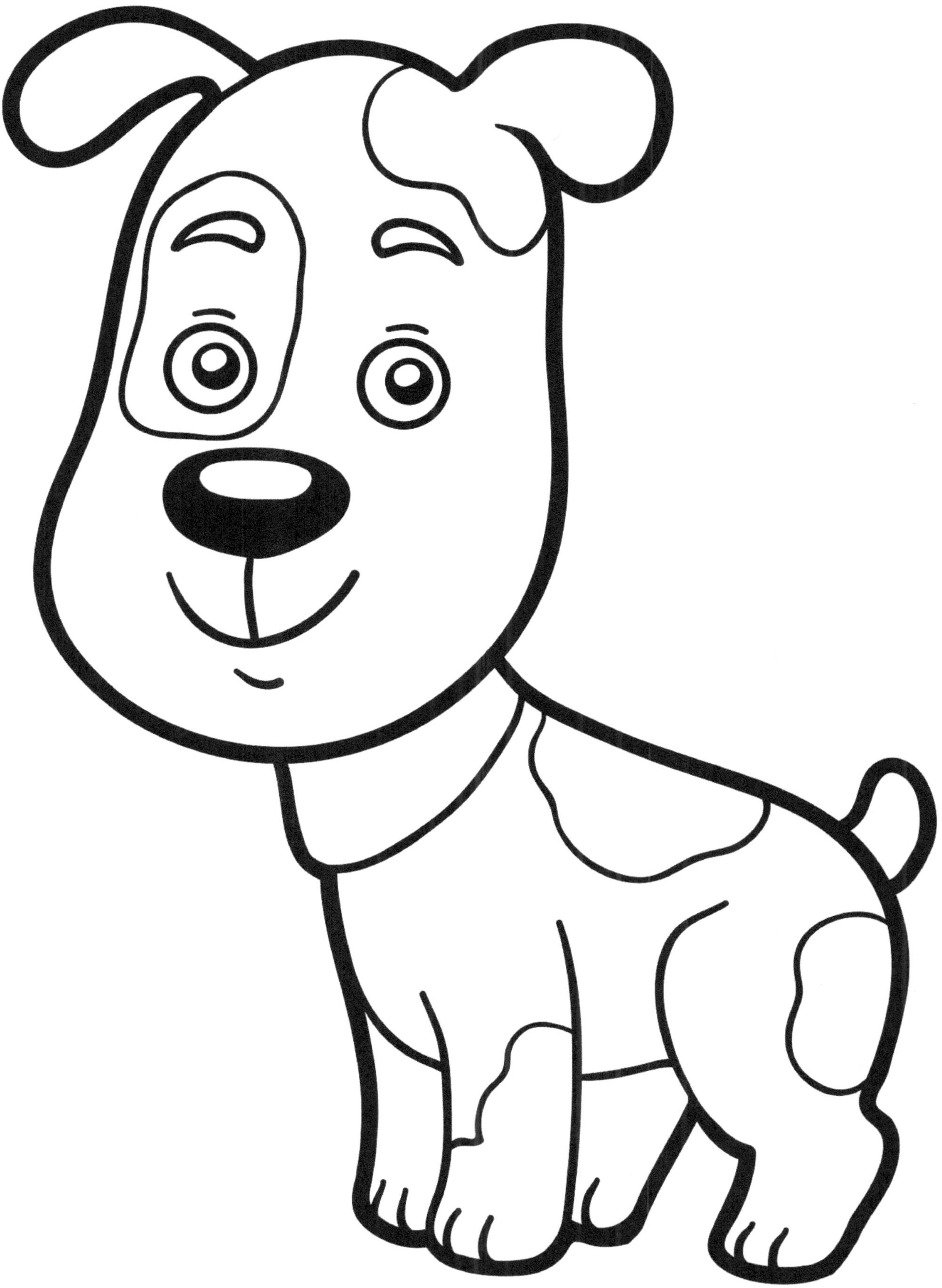

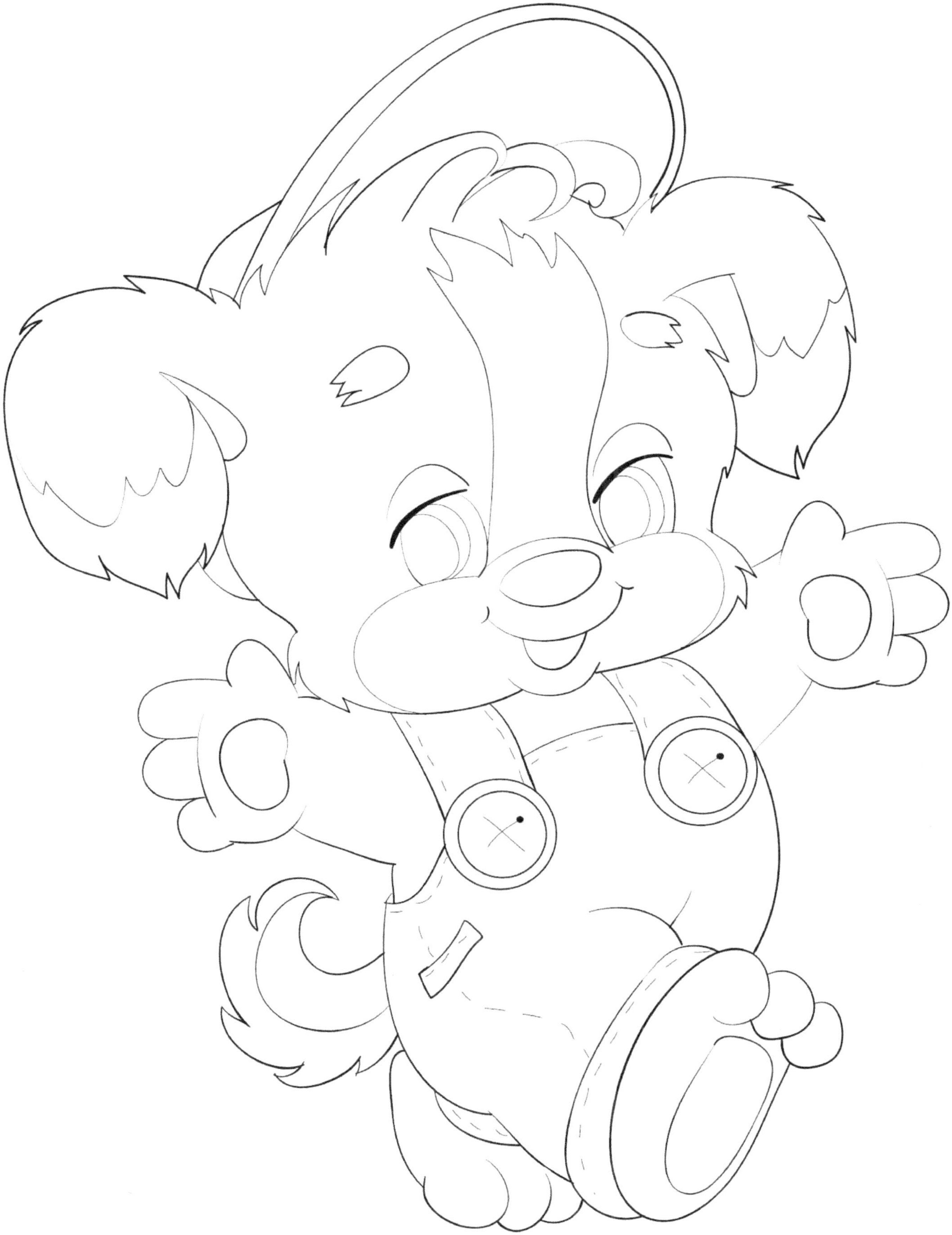

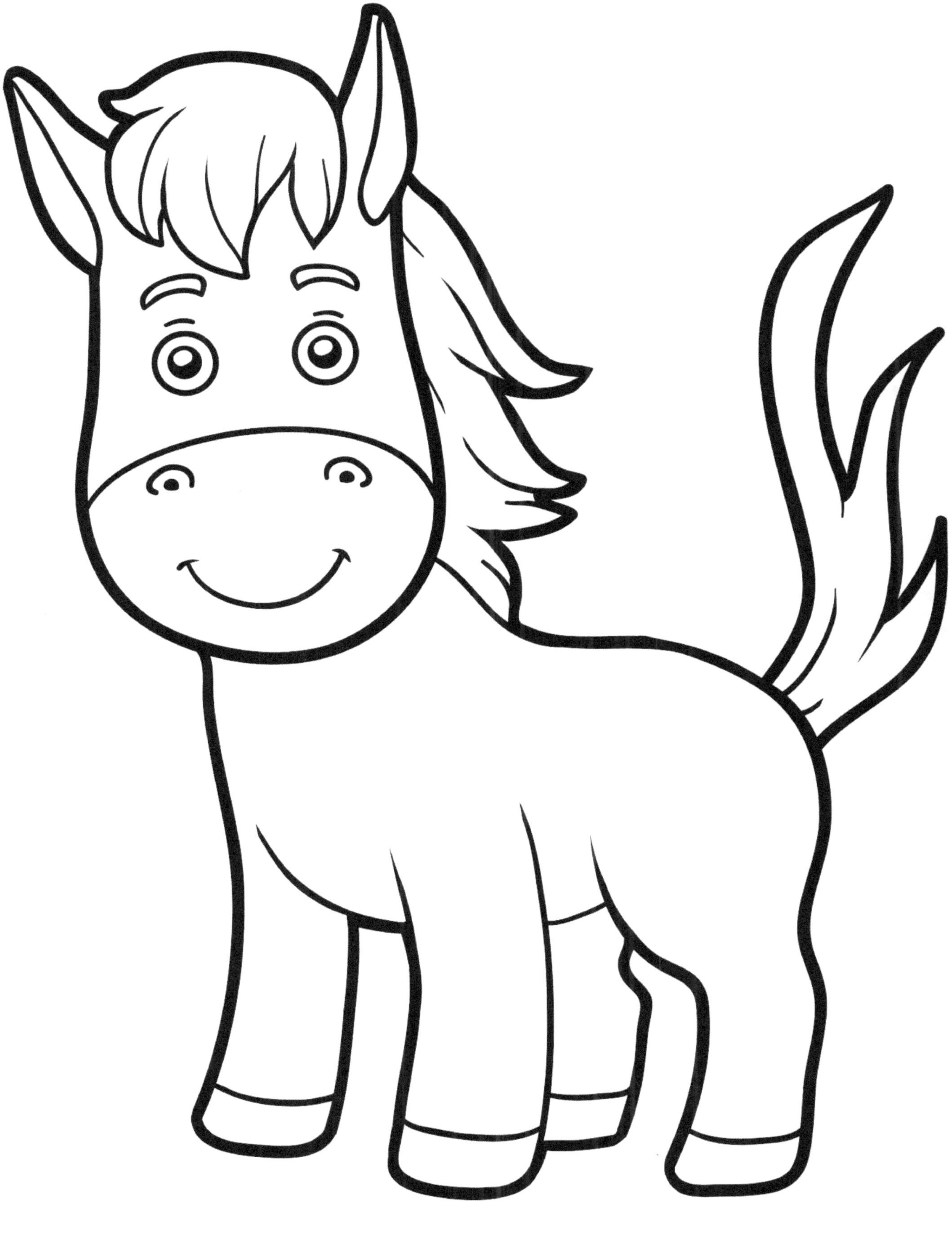

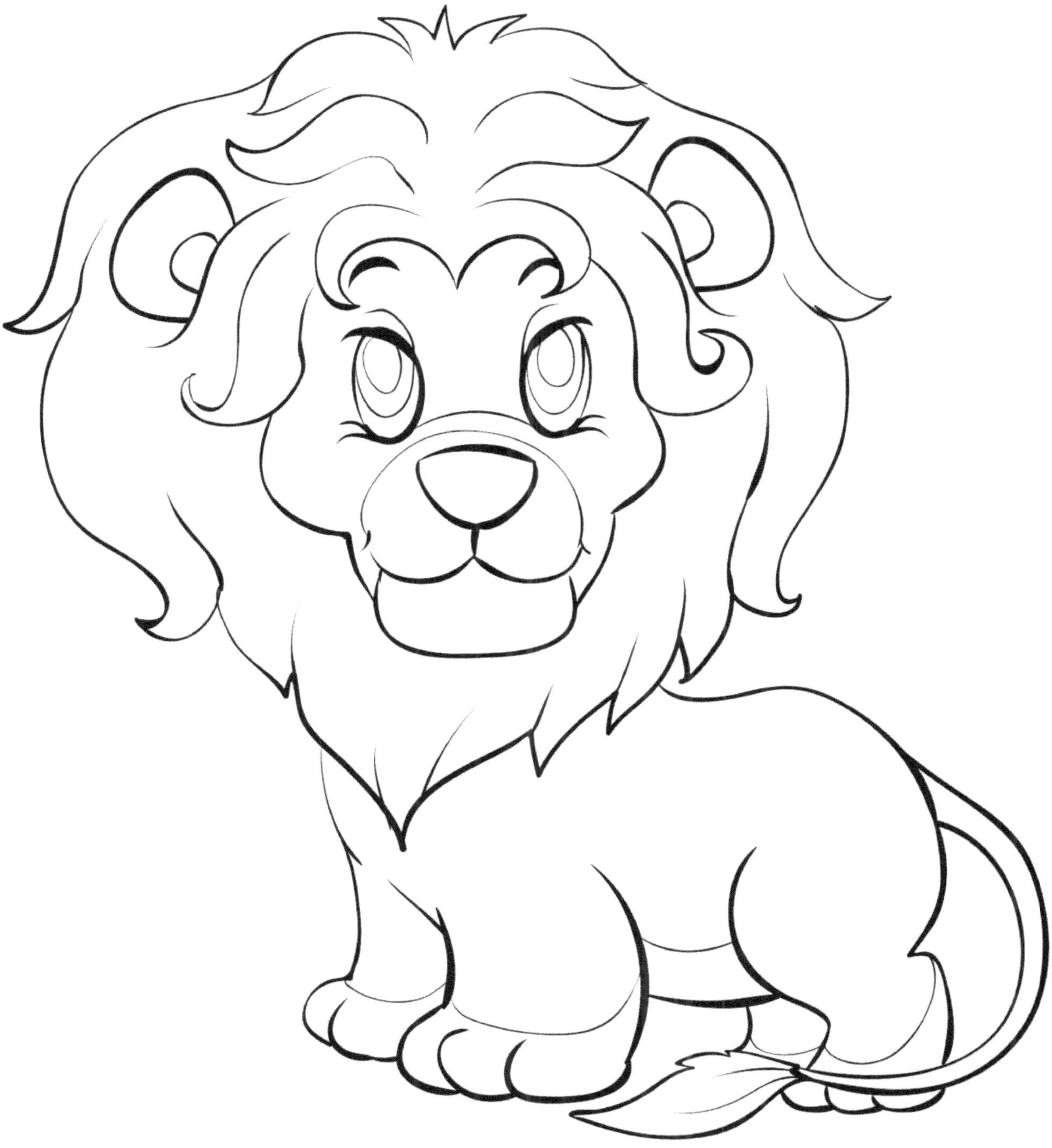

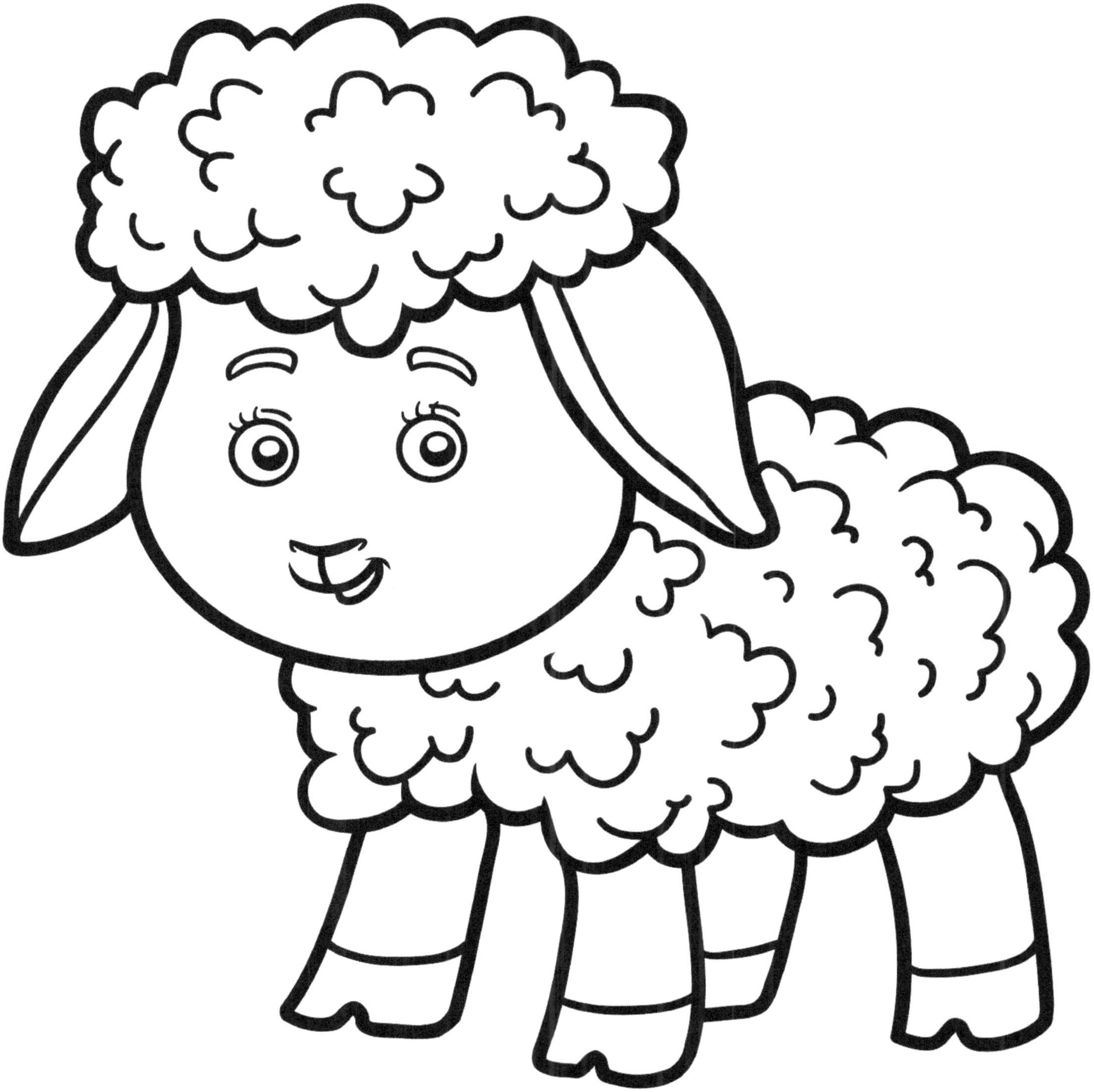

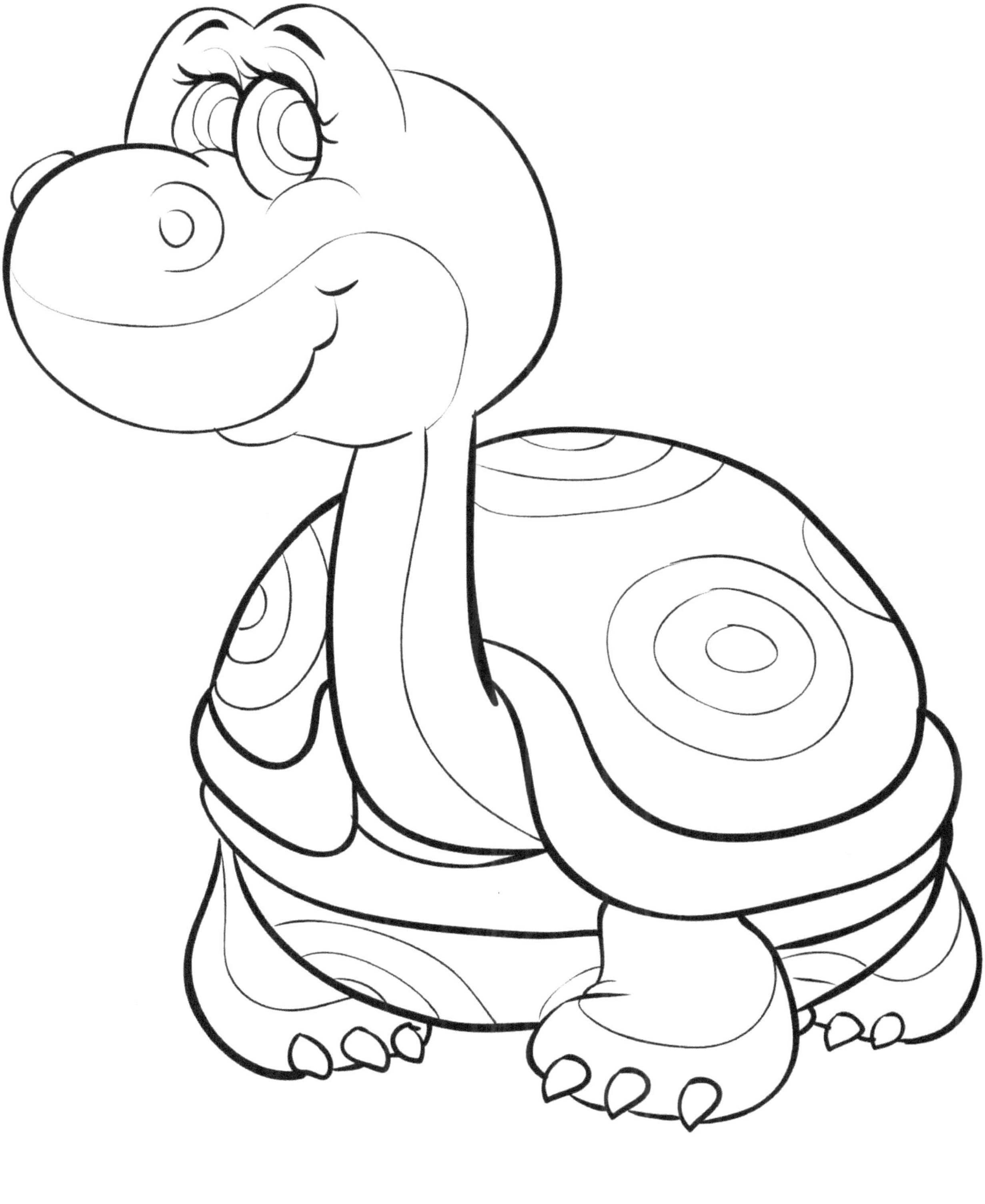

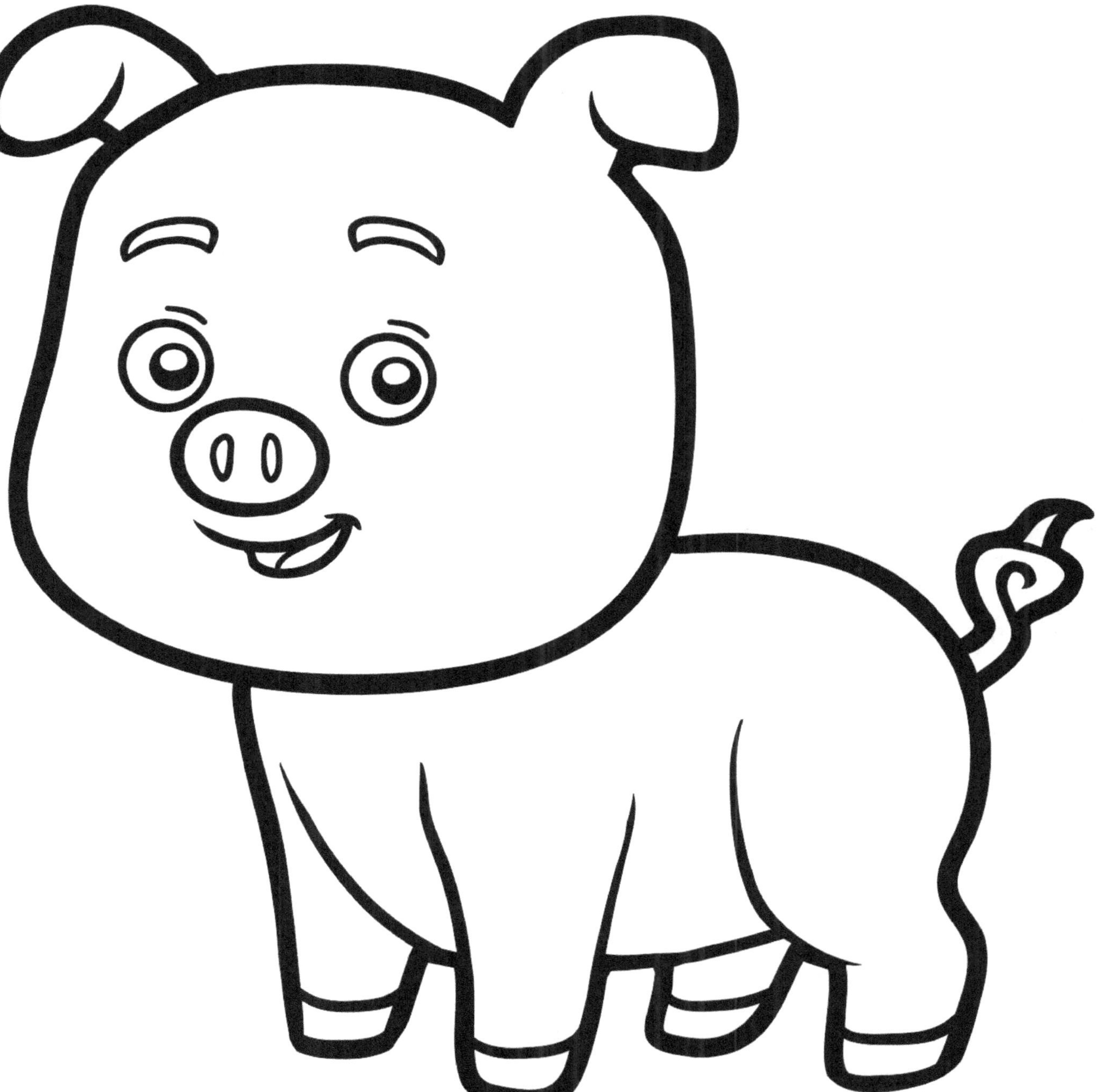

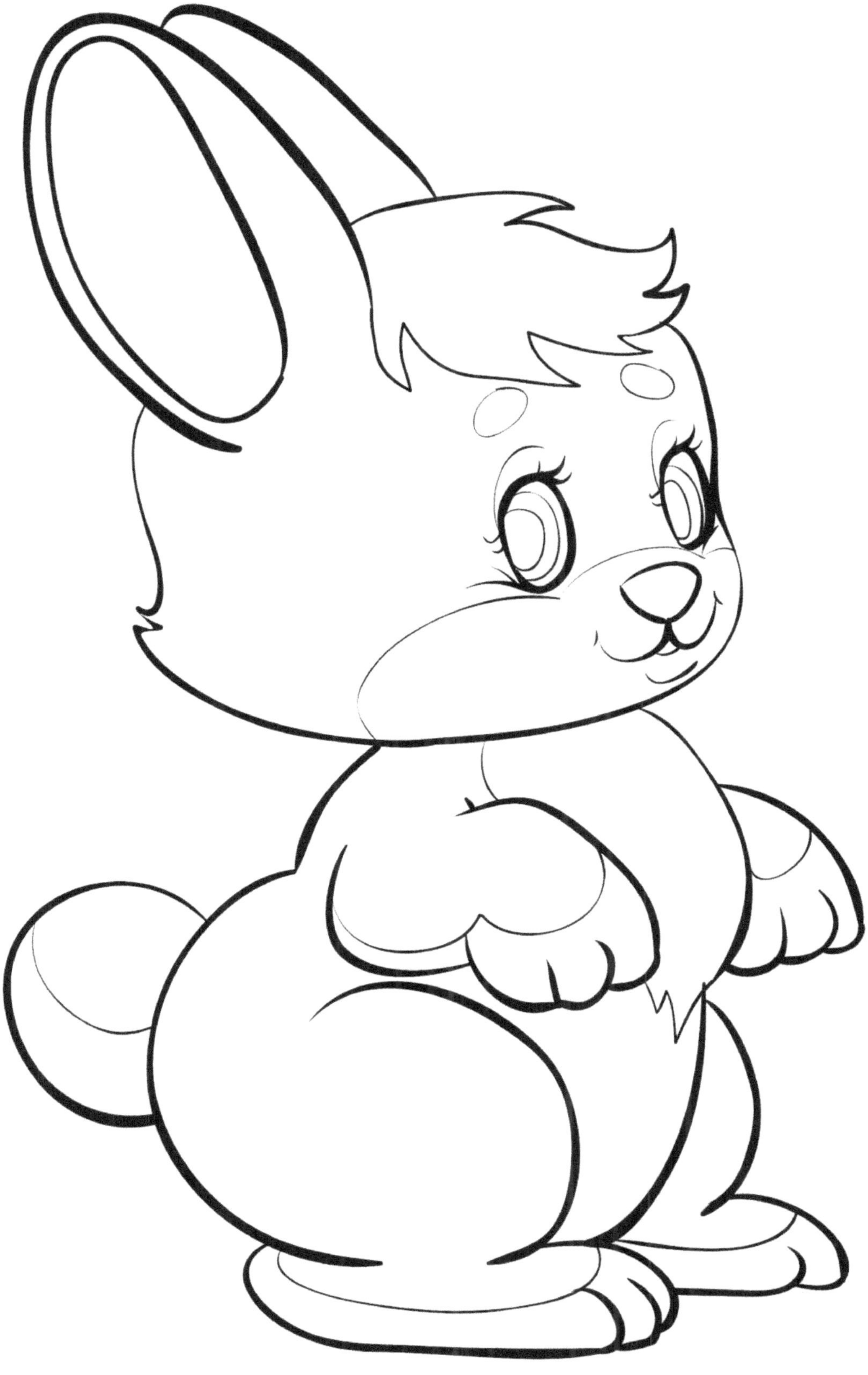

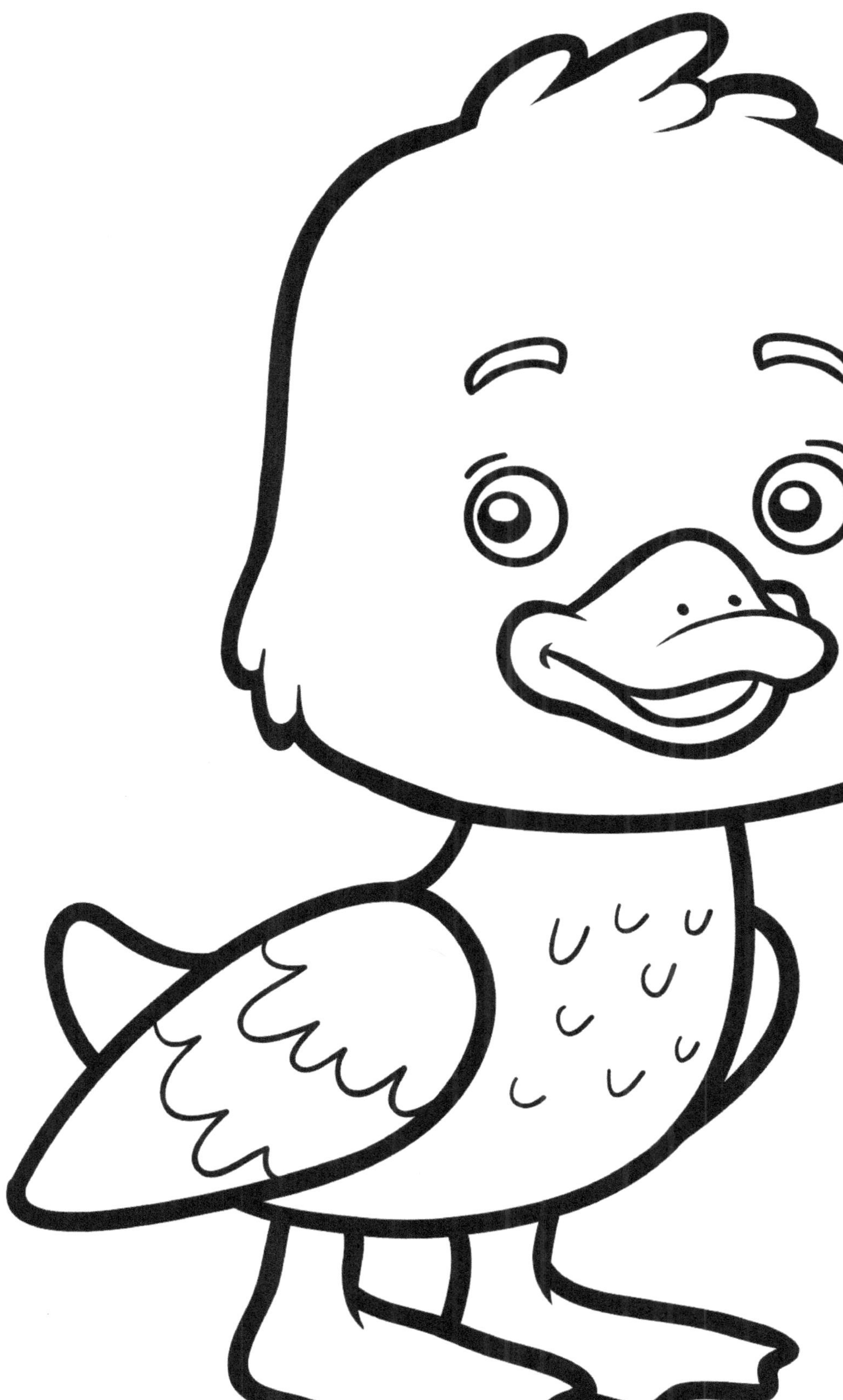

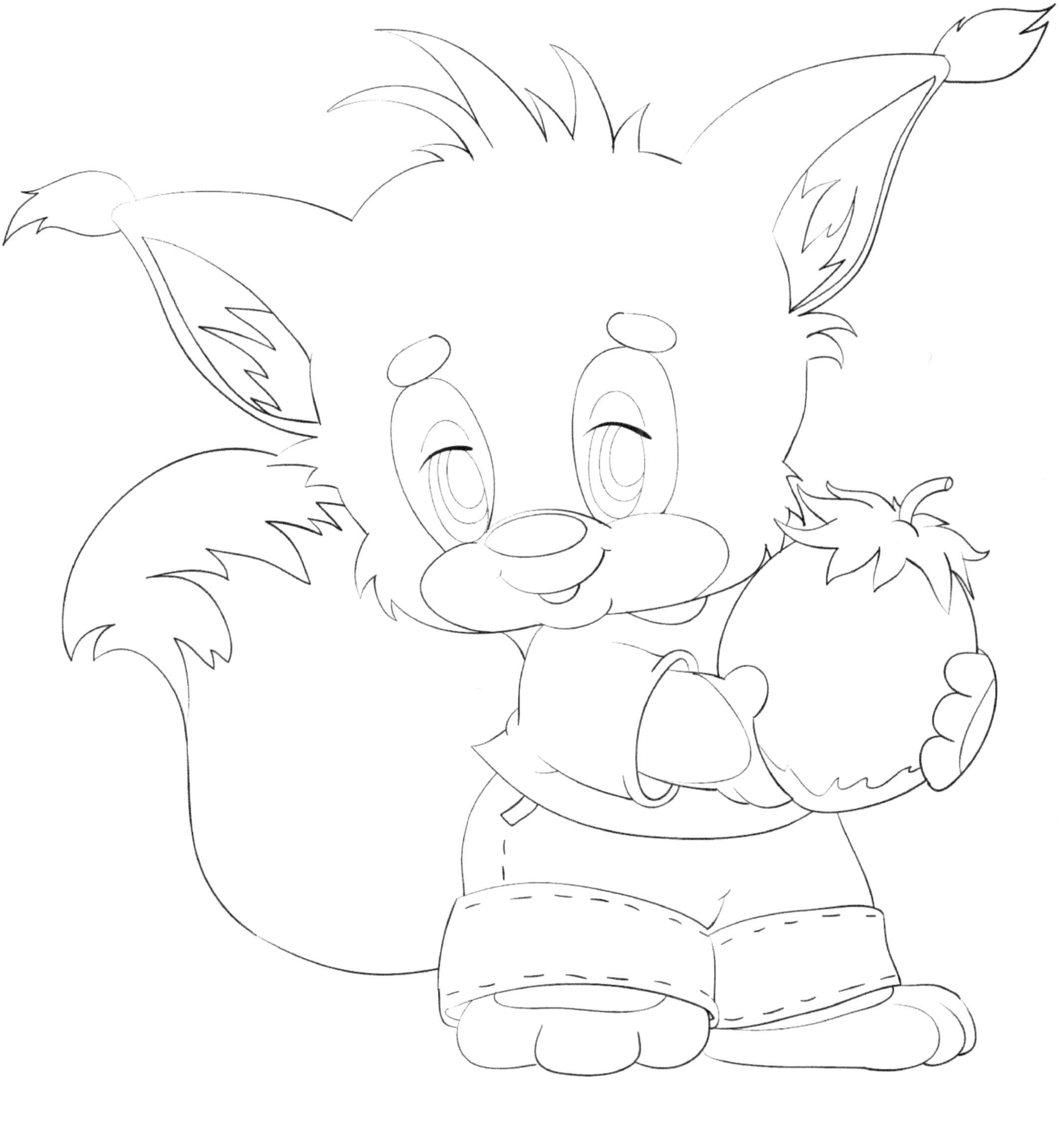

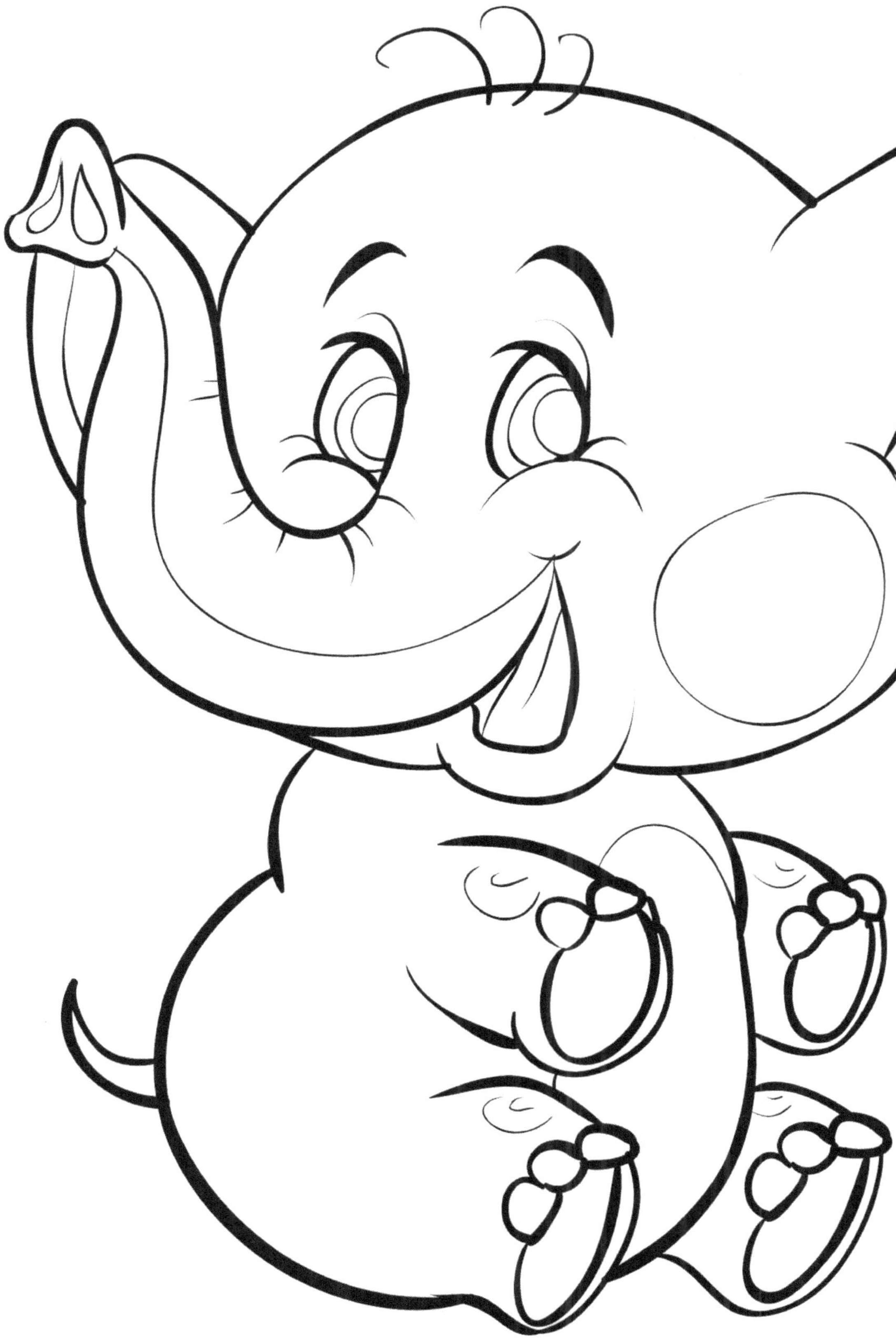

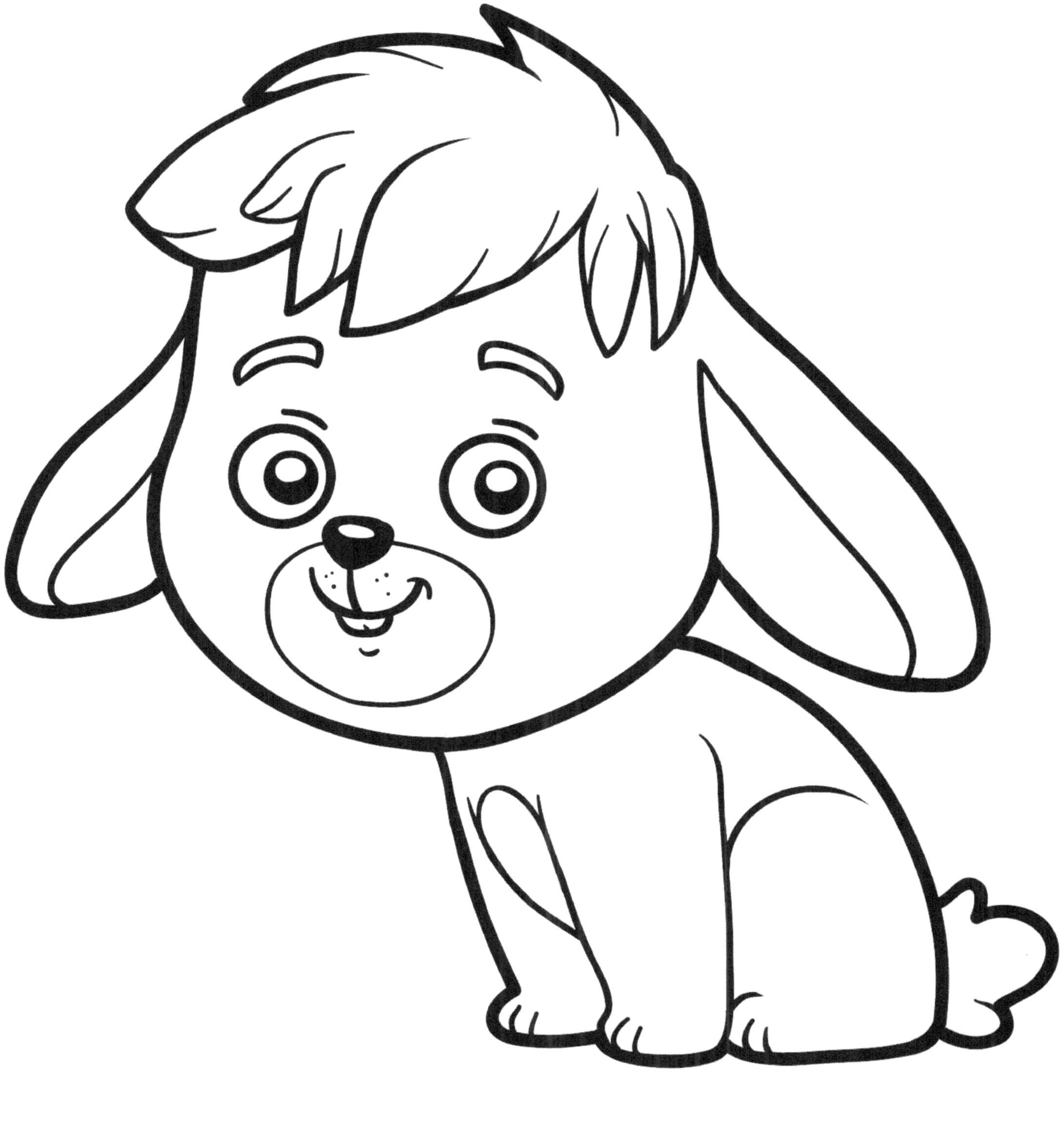

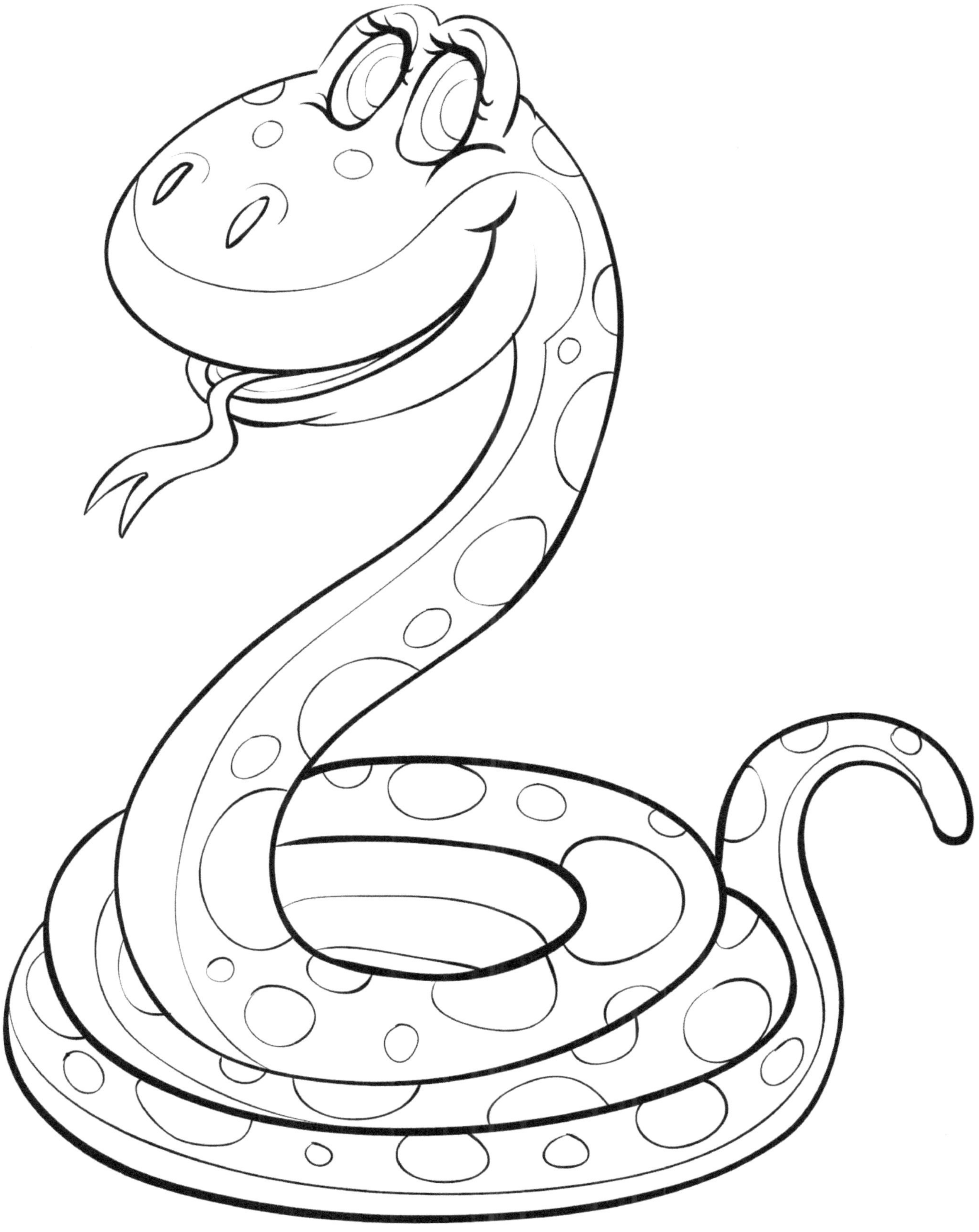

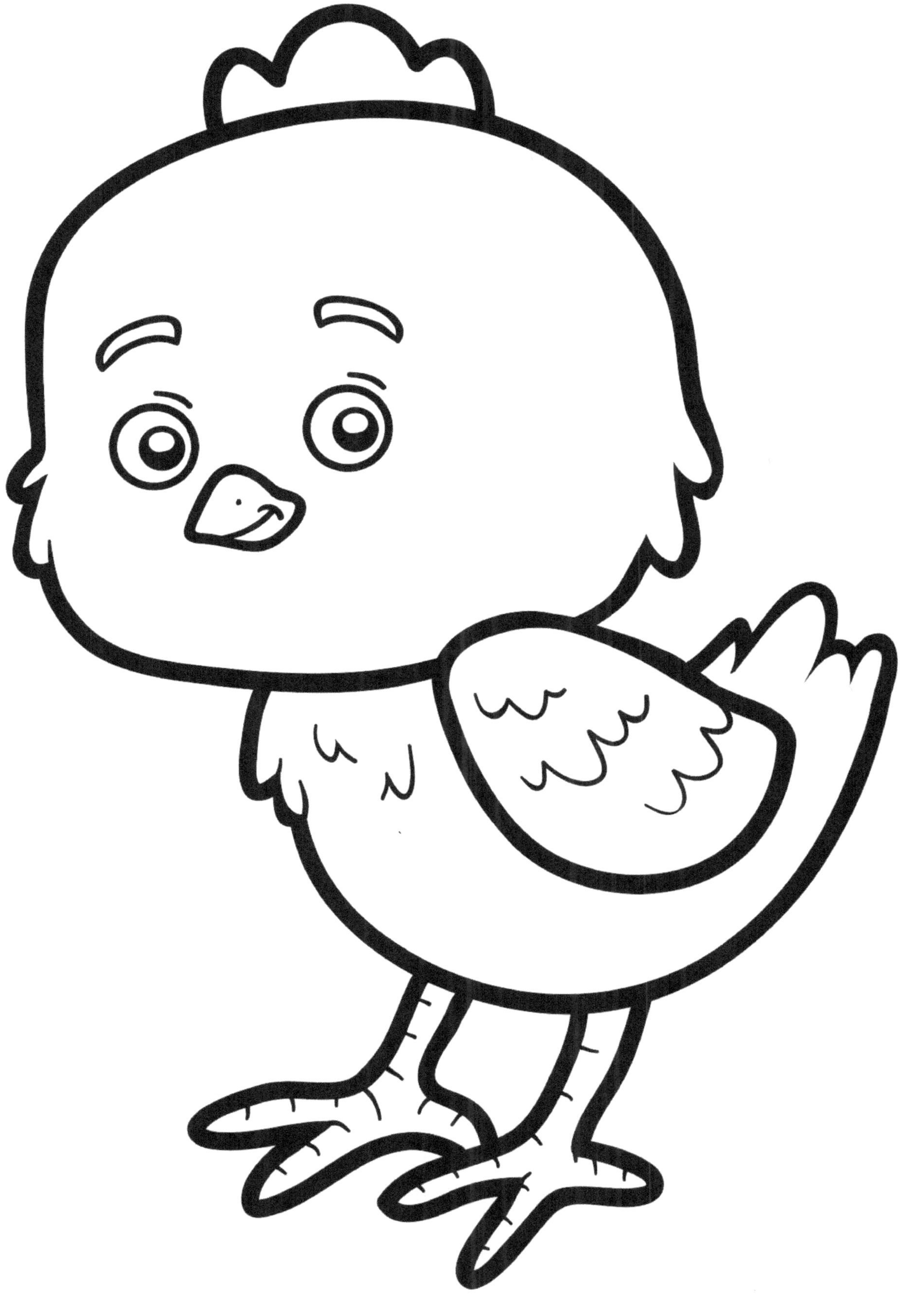

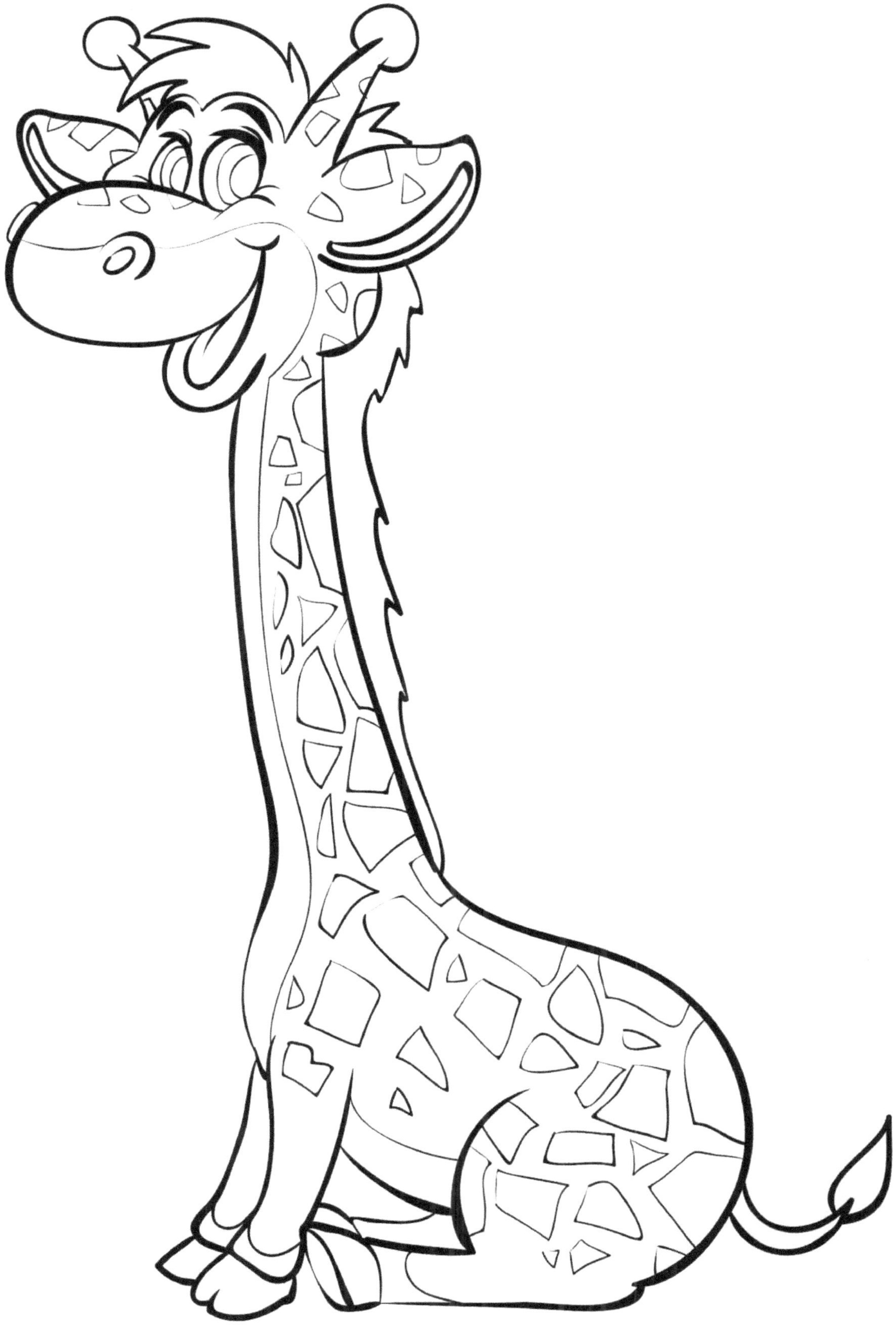

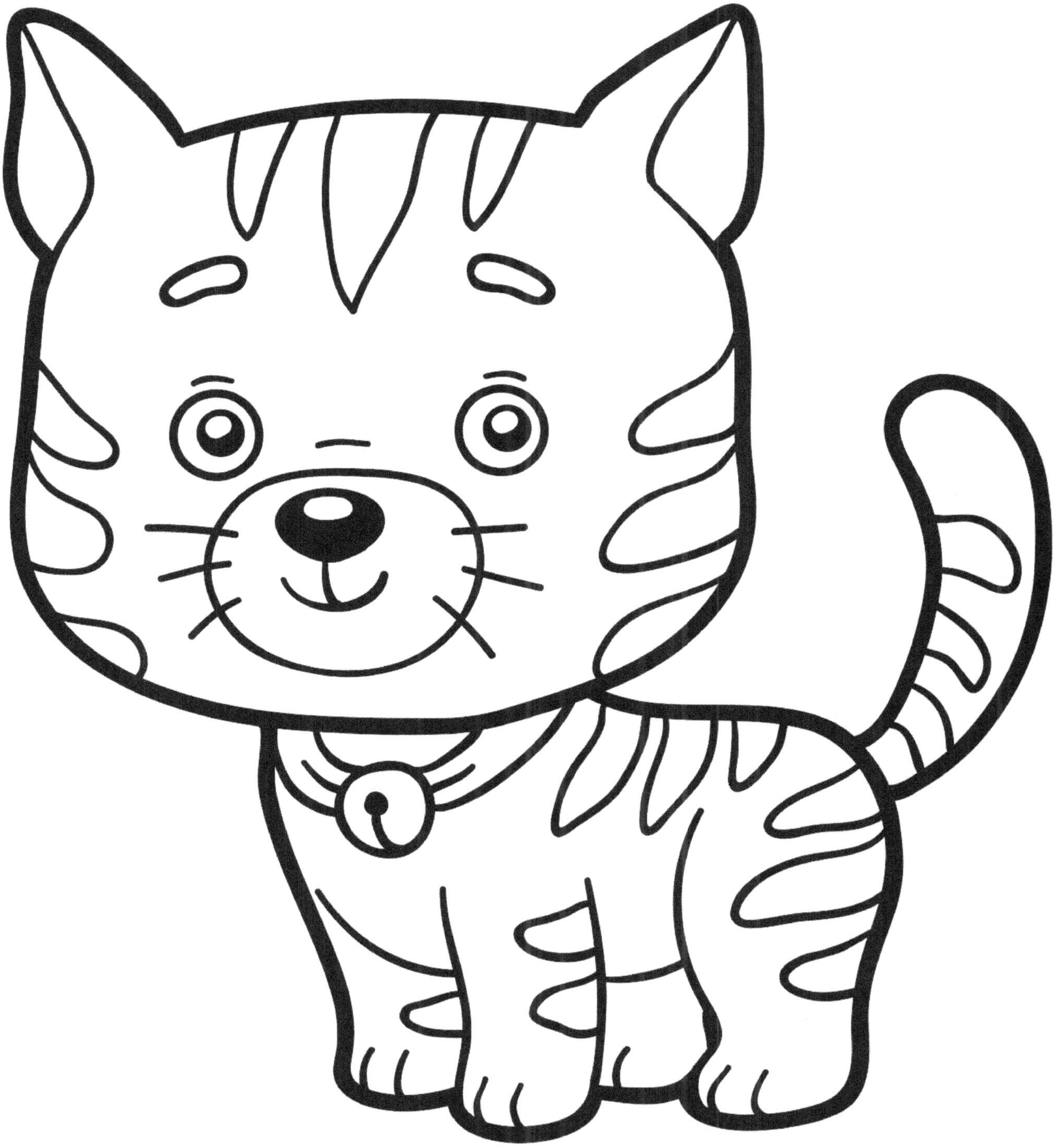

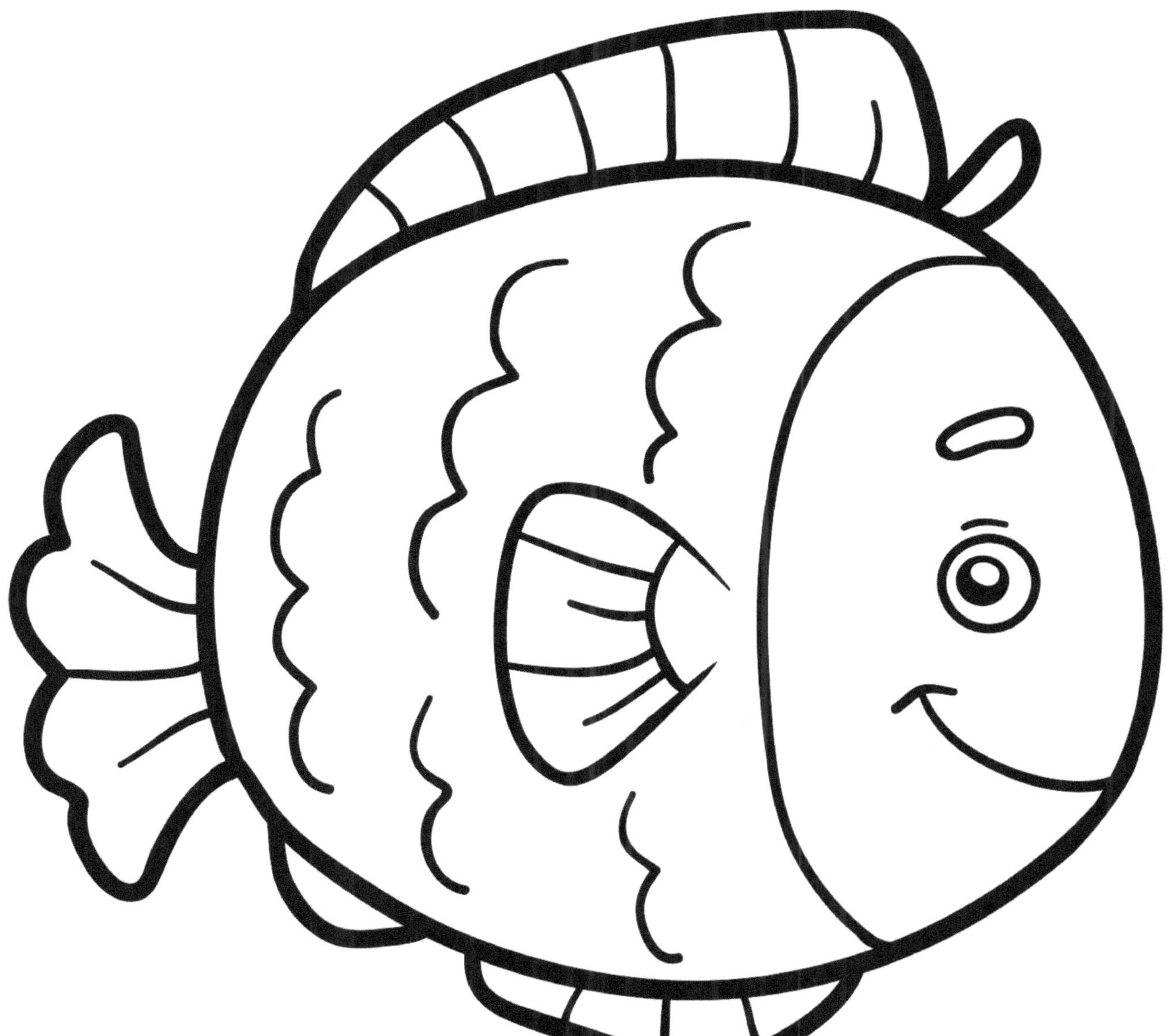

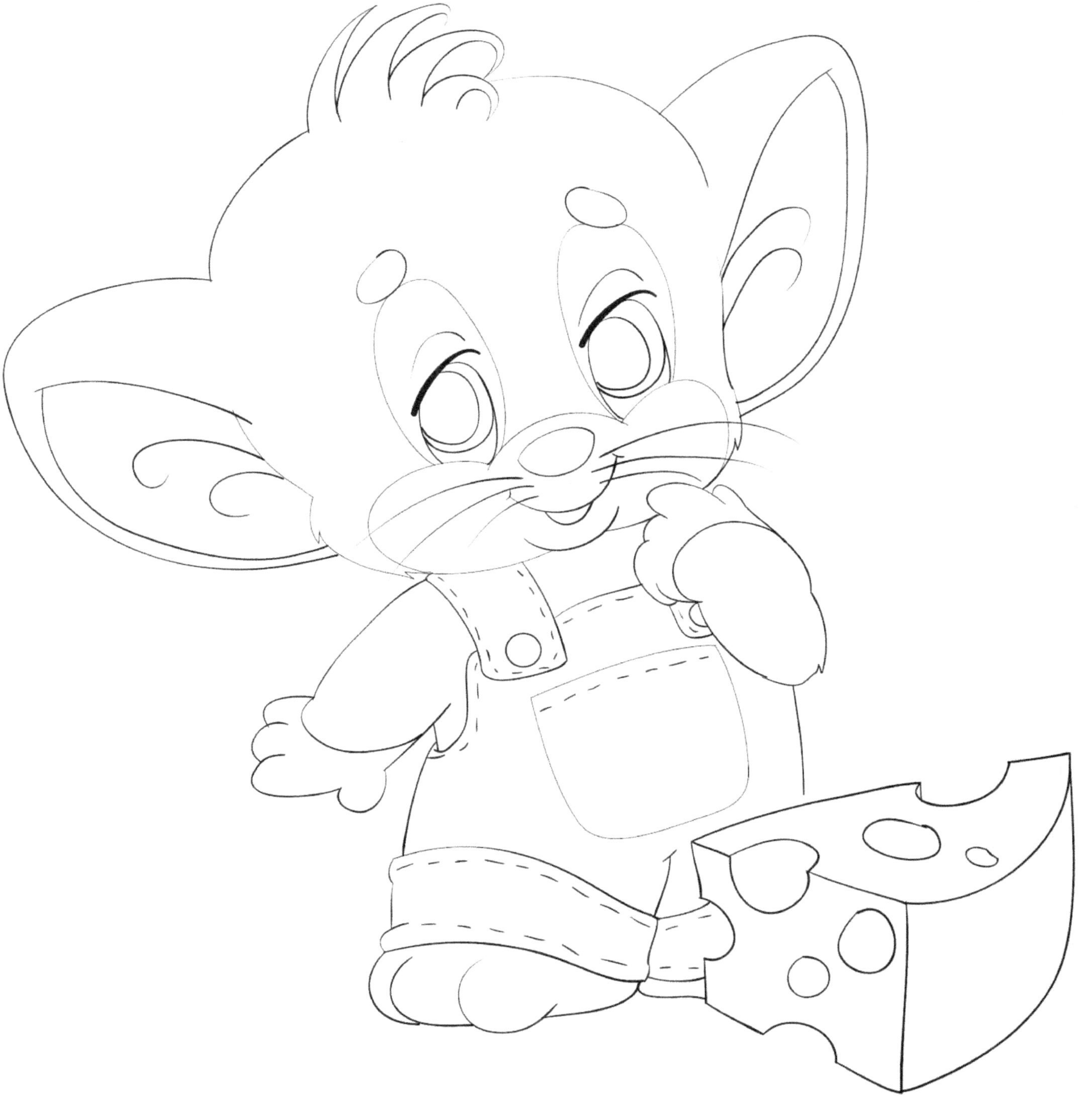

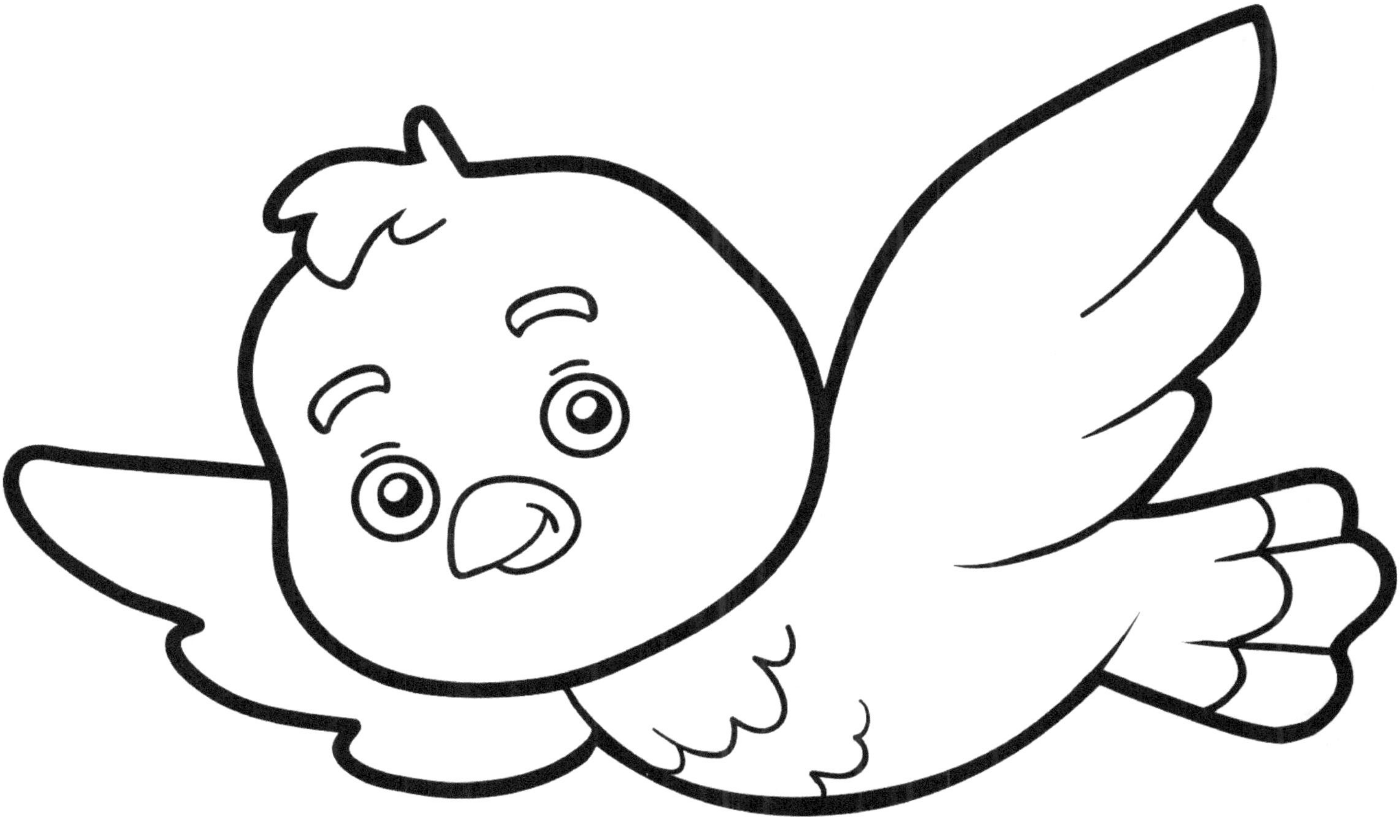

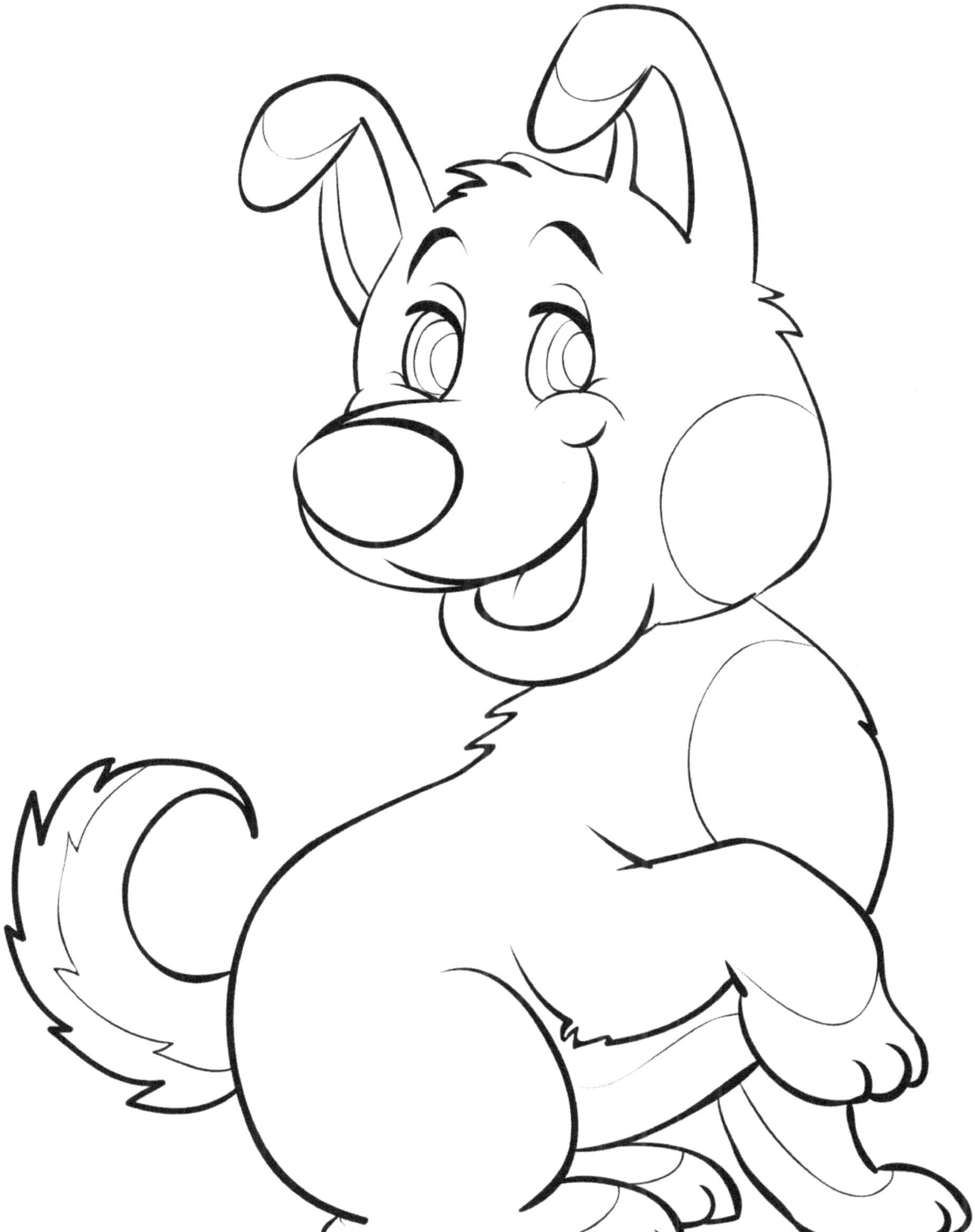

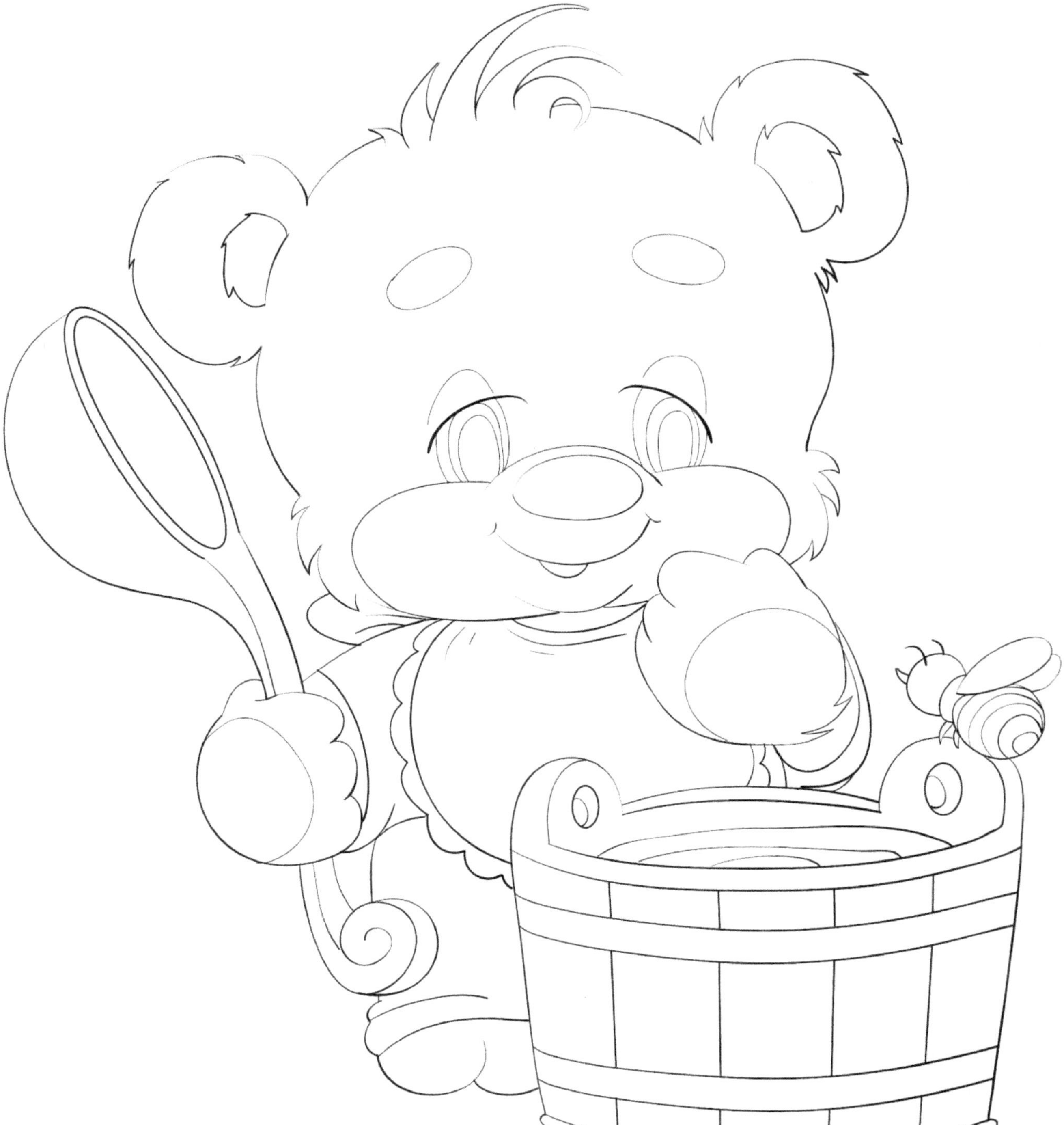

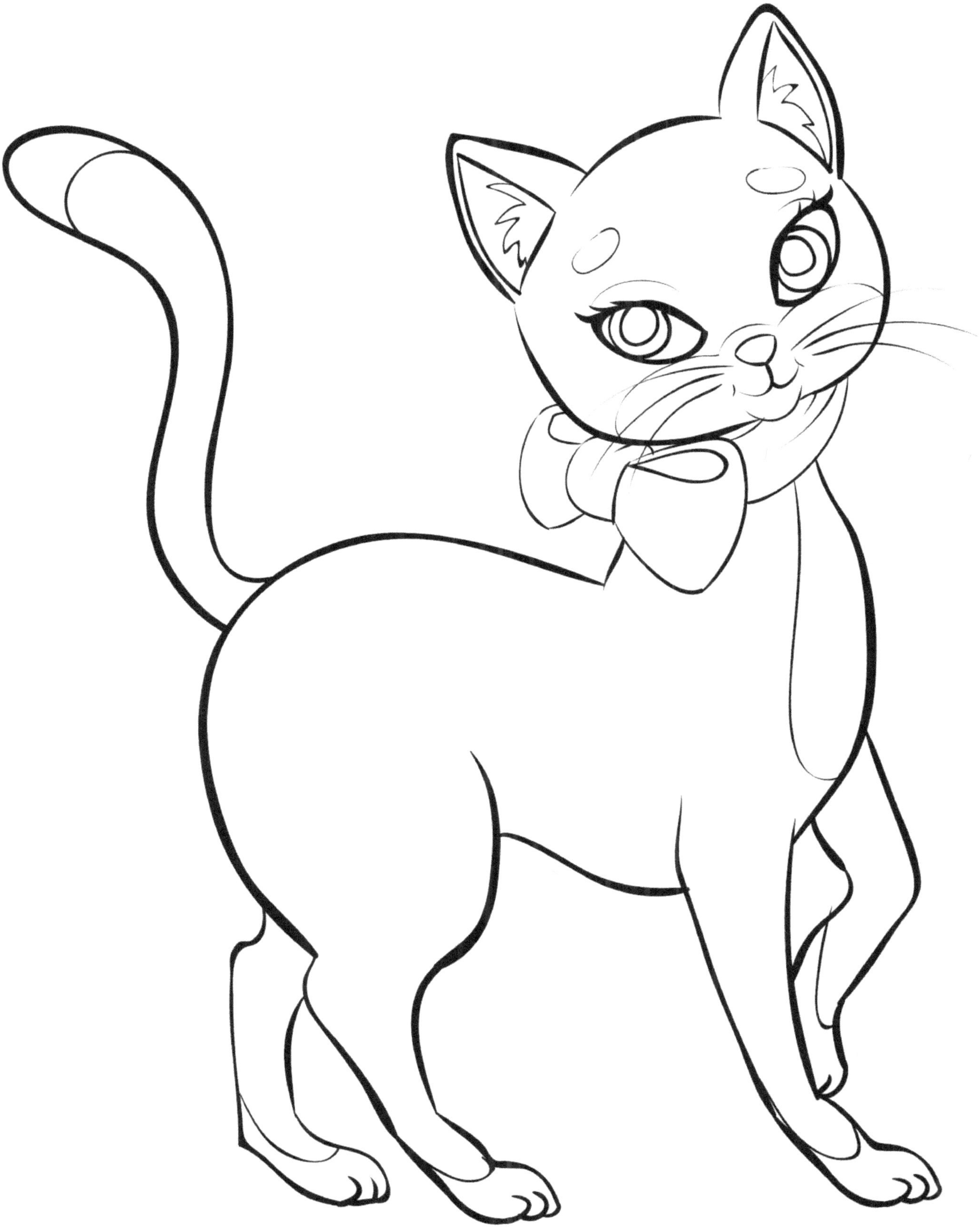

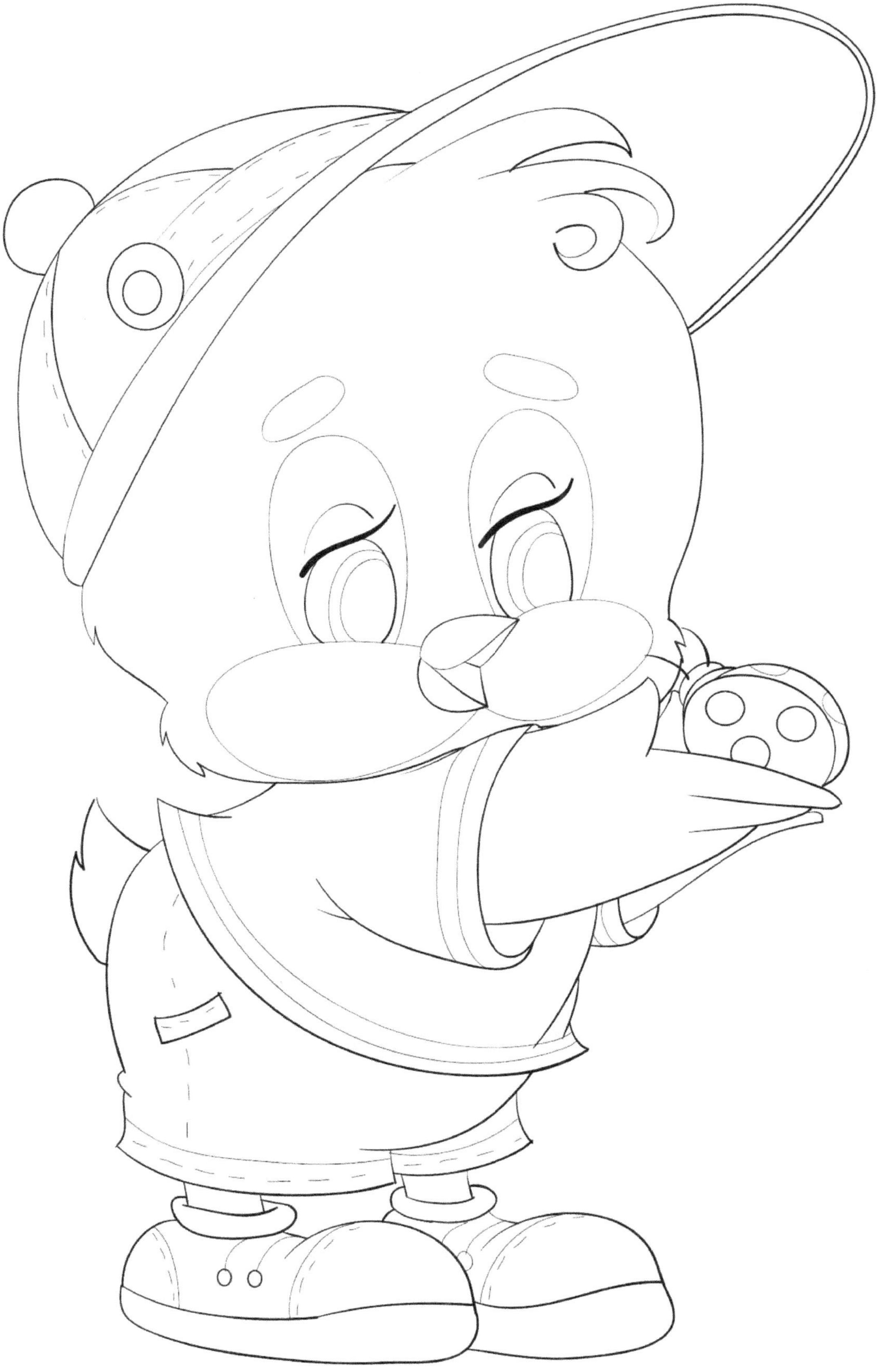

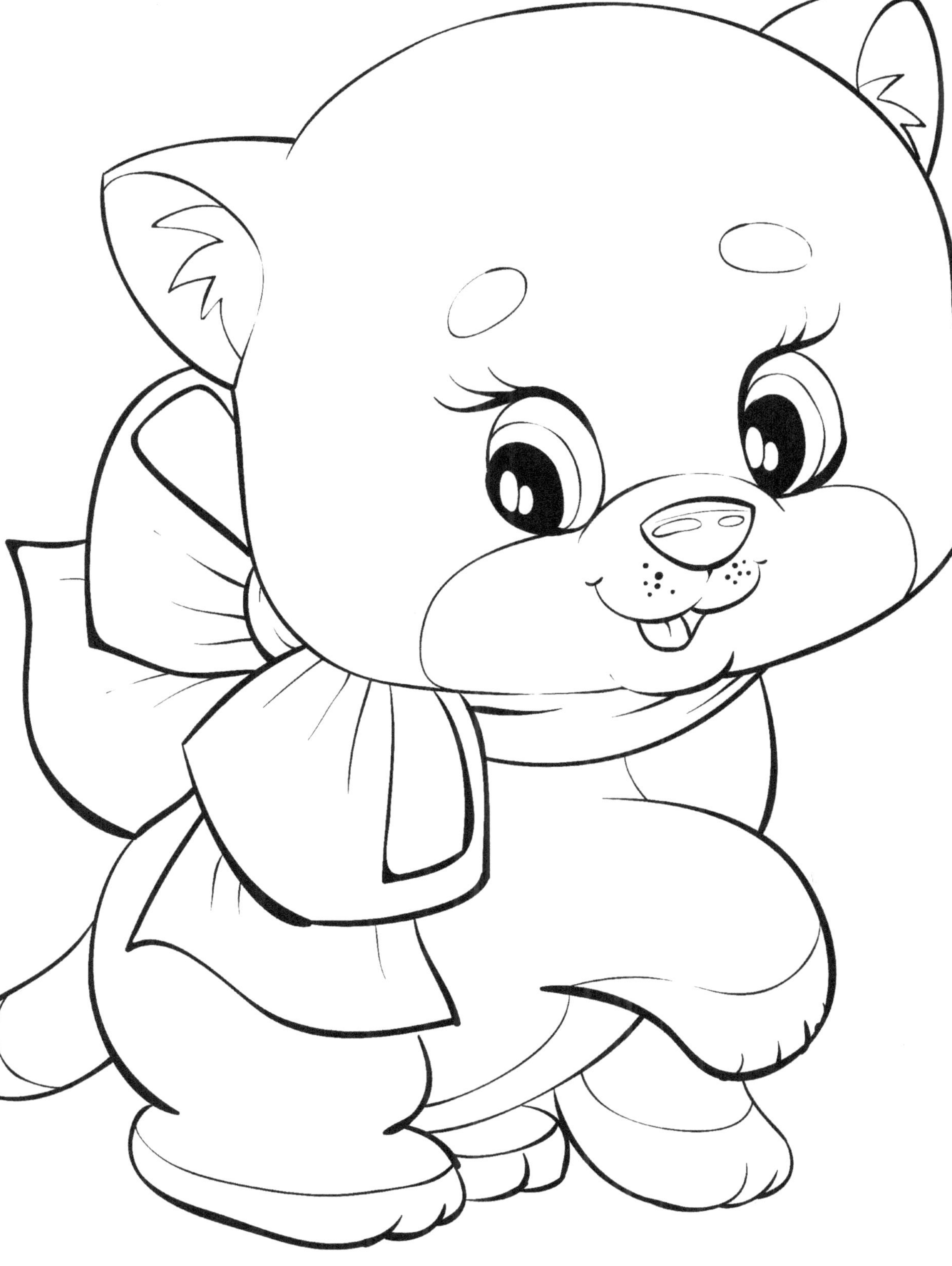

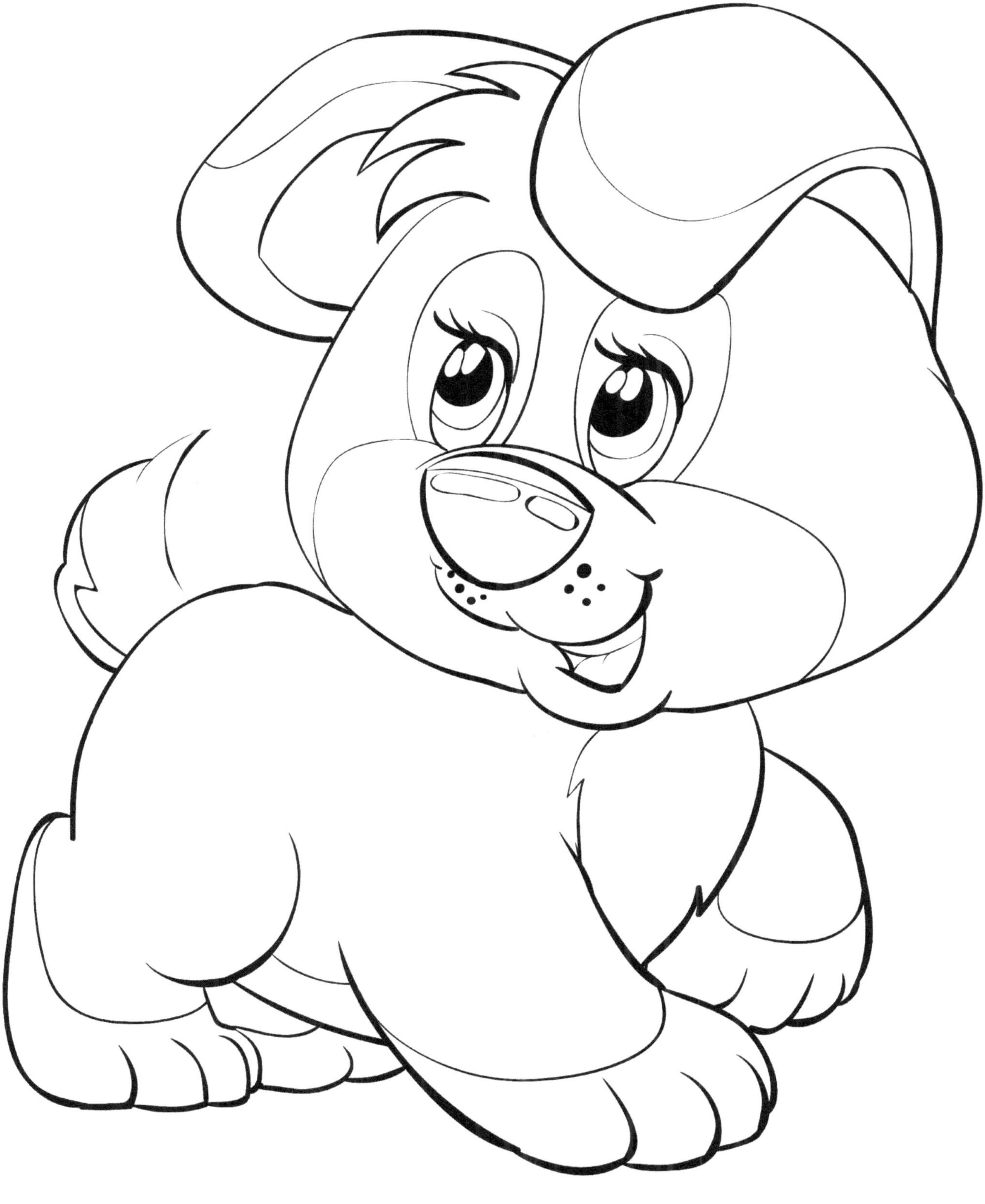

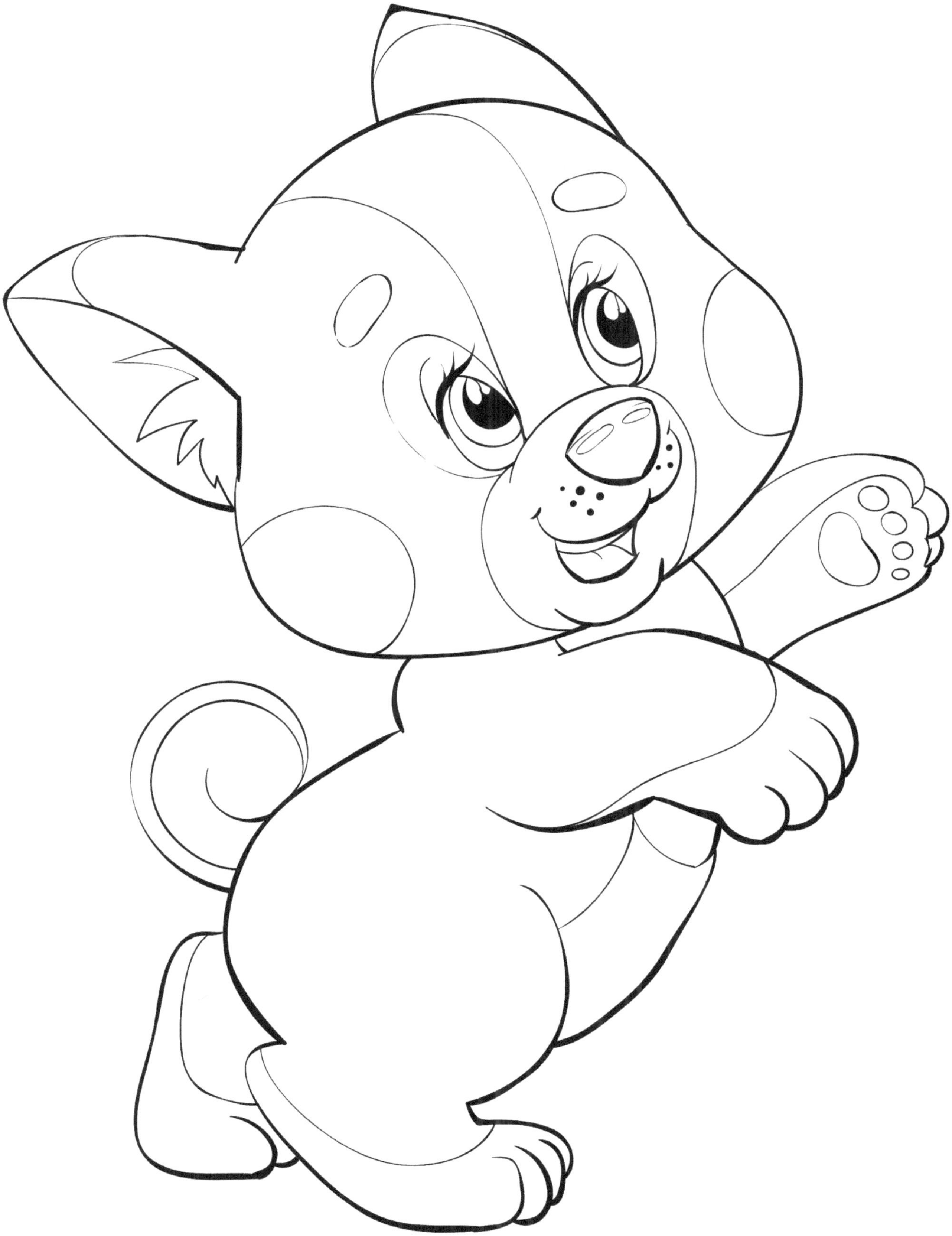

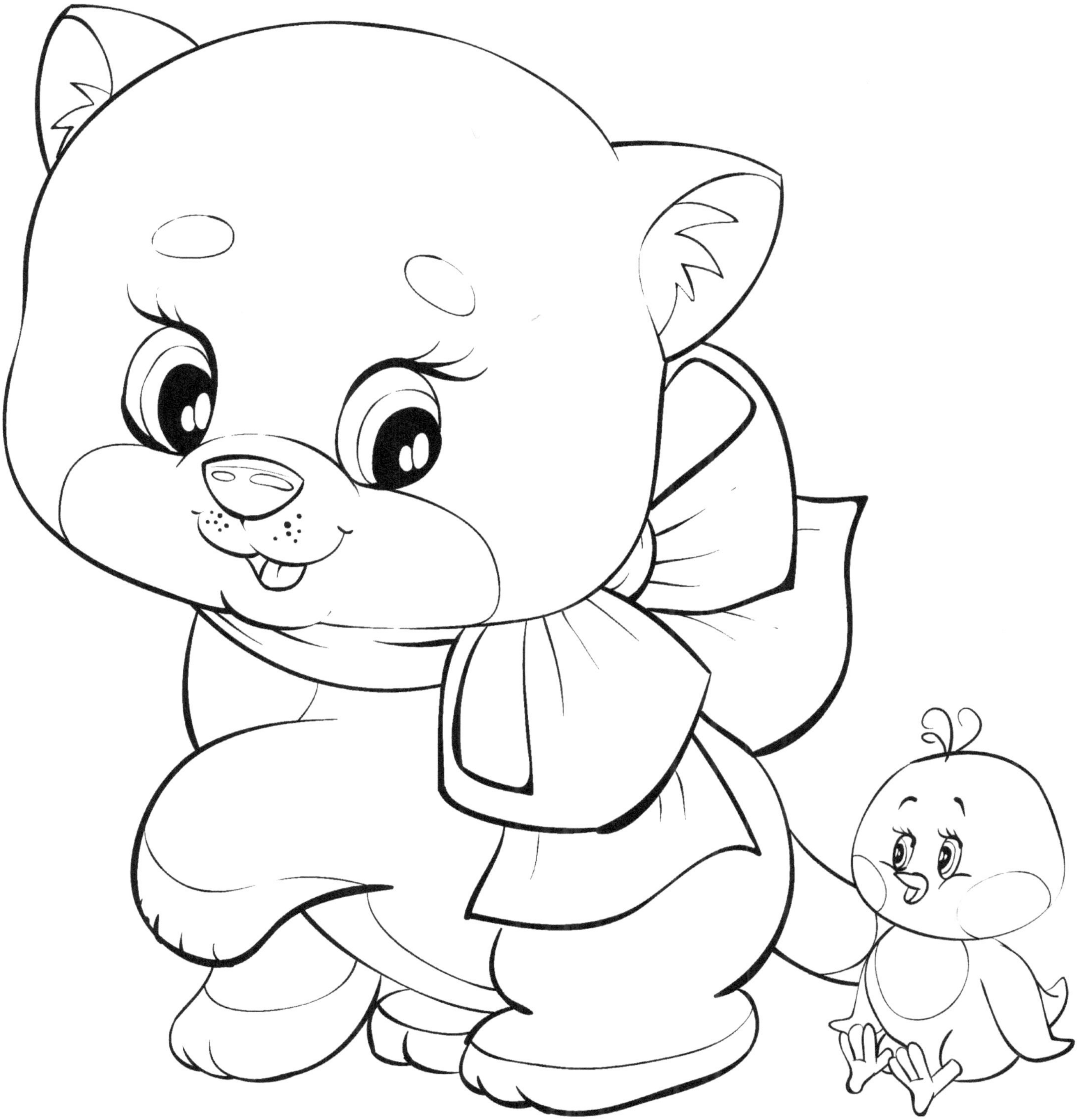

www.ingramcontent.com/pod-product-compliance
Lightning Source LLC
Chambersburg PA
CBHW081153280526
45787CB00008B/3316
* 9 7 8 1 5 4 8 8 1 7 0 8 4 *